era.

/ˈɪərə/

noun

a long and distinct period of history.
the end of one is the death of an [era].
for me that was for twitter,
and threads, where i found my rhyme, again,
was the start of a new one in 2023.

similar

epoch, age, time.

Haider Bahrani

Copyright © 2024 Haider Bahrani
All rights reserved.

mongrelhybrid.com

to
vicky
amelia
stephanie
♥

Contents

*these poems were originally written on micro blogging
site @threads each a little bit of the day's story and
presented in reverse chronology*

*again each was written and these were my rules ad hoc
and in less than a minute or two*

*there is some light touch editing mostly in the first five
minutes and a little bit as i put them together here for you*

as you can tell i've left out the punctuation mostly

that i will leave up to you

the first line of nearly all is the title too

pinned thread

when i start
a bit of verse on here
i have no idea
what i will write next
nor the context
nor when
i end

You'll see this one again

era
every one
ends
you never
quite know
not really
not when
not for a while after
even if there are
a few
false dusks
someone calls it
but things carry on
it started
with one
or two
then
it became
quite a few
and they
as if constant
carried on
till again
they were two
fanning the flame
till they
were none

coffee
or exercise
a walk in the park
a meal
a burger or curry
putting the world
in it's place
but without
much haste
as long as it's done
with two
or three
at least
a few more
maybe
but not enough for
a cacophony
can be
quite nice

it's me
can you see me?
my self
and five
or six times
today
my selfie
my confidence
it's not lost
but can you find me?
i have a reason
or maybe not
but just because
i show
or even if
i show off
why
be nasty?

is it folly
for me to
act
and not
worry?

the storm
of thoughts
overwhelming
every sense
almost always
on the morning
and sometimes
through the day
it is the norm
more often
than it is not

disarmed
by what is
and what is not
human
alarmed
by how we care
for the life of one
and how we show none
for the death of a ton
is it colour?
is it kin?
or
is it simply
fear of saying
the wrong thing?

poetry
it's expected
in words
but
i have heard
a painting
dancing
a picture
the movement
of objects
subjects
and that
of the birds
the sound
the sense
the scent
not just
how
we put them
in verse

news
who decides
what to say
when at 7am
my alarm
starts my day?
will it align
my thoughts
this way
or that?
will it decide to
make me
angry
or not?

excited

we are very excited
yet we deliver it
monotone
well most of us
excepting those of us
under the age of thirteen
when excited is what
then
we truly mean

the train
it left
without me on it
not sure
i even bought a ticket
it was the fast train
to somewhere
i'd prefer
to take my time
getting there
when the journey ends
it ends
so i'm in no hurry
to find out
what's round that bend
i'm happy
to be here
for a bit
or a lot
the people here are good
what if ahead
they're not?
and somewhere
may be nice
but sometimes
it's nice to stay
at some of the places
on the way

ok
i've only got
five minutes
i mean
to do this
time only
takes it's time
when life is a grind
but mine
is beating double time
making four
and a bit minutes
out of nine

i have
lots of questions
like
if we just function
why do we need to be?
but most of all
why do
we
not live in trees?

meaningless poetry

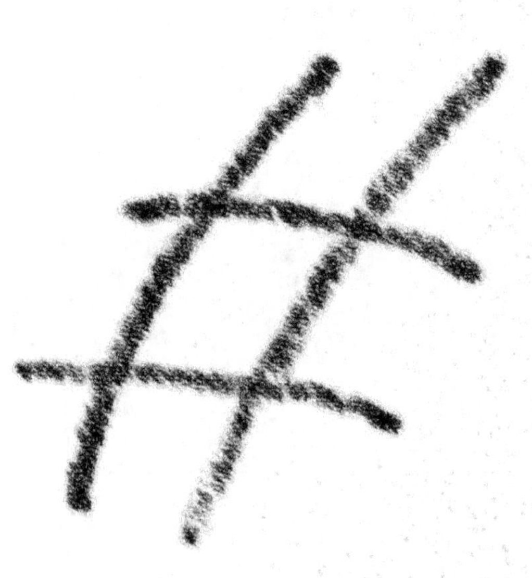

a lot to do
i know
i do
i could start
not sure where
but there's
a cup of tea to be made
if i ask
someone else will
want one too
so then
i'll have to

we are free
unless
we impede
the money tree

when i write
songs
and other stuff
i write a lot of it
most of it not fit
but i don't stop
i put out some
i record some
i carry on
guitar by my side
note pad and pen
i even type things
now and then
it's more than breathing
and i
don't think i will ever
be done

a wave
not a flood
it passed
it was small
i'm not even wet
not at all
like so many things
that pass
they leave little or no impress
often maybe
actually
it is a flood
lots of little bits
we walk through them
like we do mist

more noise
there is money
to be made
just to distract
yet
we embrace the escape

viking day
the day they landed
all of us
well back then
were just prey
not people
a child would treat
a cuddly toy better
they came to plunder
but let's be honest
do we
these days
behave
that much better?

the sun
is shining on my screen
i can't see much
to write
i could move
but the sun
it's warm
it's bright
it makes me feel nice
so you can
have the dark night
and write
as i sleep
i'll take
the sun

i tried
to write a story
in prose
like the pro's
but every other line
i rhythmed
and i lost focus
when i saw a butterfly
or was it
oh i meant to do
that thing
there's something
flashing on my phone
then reached
for my snack
my coffee
and
i'm still
holding my pen
while typing
what?
i don't know
and
i can't
remember
why?!

do you remember?
when writing an email
was considered
so cool
it was with
a typewriter thing
with a screen
and without
a spool
it was wow!
i don't need paper
a stamp
to post it
as a letter
you wrote it
and seconds later
it's there
do you remember?
no?
was it really
that long ago?

if everything we do
is a sell
where is our soul?
if everything we do
is to appeal
how are we whole?
the hole
that is marked
the one that
we long to fill
the time that passes
when we are too busy
too tired or ill
then when
the time comes
we find ourselves
tired again
and too old
so we hope
for our children
to fill their own
but then
their time
passes
as well

it works
i plugged it in
and it's quite a thing
it does stuff
a while back
you'd never imagine
i pressed this
and connected that
then i left it
i carried on
and when i came back
well ok
it didn't quite
do it all
but over all
back in the day
it would have taken
several of us
and at least one
with a specialist degree
to do this
i mean that's
for anyone over 50
the younger ones
can do all of this
twice as quick
with an app

the mince pies
they're almost
gone
all the fuss
that makes us
happy
over friendly
warm inside
but mostly
anxious
is done
back to
work
the diet
the promise to more often run
and the school run
the mince pies
i ask
anyone
else
want the last one?

it's night
i've said
to the kids
sleep tight
they smiled
said
night night
and love you daddy
now i might
too once
i've read
the news
sleep i hope
till it's bright

to most
to make it
through the day
is a boast
the fight is not to grow
but keep you
and your children alive
sheltered
fed
hopefully educated
then you hope they grow
but
by the time
it's their time
we put everything
in their way
while they're
in their prime
debt
trouble
yes a few are blessed
but even they
have to wade through
usually the mess
the last champion
of the people left
they sold a belief
and we placed a bet
and to them
we remain
in debt

cold hands
cold feet
lips are so numb
i can't
properly speak
i've been outside
the birds
the trees
honestly
what a treat

coffee
if i hadn't had
the last one
i'd probably be
asleep now
but this is fun
wide awake
reading poems
about frivolous things
deep thinking
and of course
perennial
heart ache
and
not forgetting
what people
have had
for tea

eventually
as normally
for me
it's easy
but sleep i did
even the kids didn't
wake me
till noon
though that was
too soon
and i'm drinking
coffee

written the following day

an avalanche
of words
inside my head
each one coming
from something
i thought or
i or someone
said
i could write it
or type it
i should keep
a pad and pen
near my bed
as i do my desk
but not everywhere
i rest
so not everything
is recorded
perhaps that's good
as some is sordid
but even when i rush
to type or sketch
the last thing
and things i thought
before
i forget
so i do
but not always
only when
i have
the chance

a flood
of mainly hope
but despair
has not
with its fellow madness
eloped
in this case
human kindness
has shown its face
in the face
of the worst parts
of the human race
if it's to atone
or natural empathy
in its normal tone
it matters not
for
we got there

i think
i will never write
not another
poem
or a song
5 mins gone
and it's done
one or the other
another one

the creator
on social media
are you
the curator
of your own media?
or have you
handed over
your personality
for someone
else to be?
is it success
verses
authenticity?
truly
can anyone else
be truly
me?

i was sold
i called to ask
why and what
i was told
not an issue
sign on the dots
i said
are you sure
this comes with the cure?
yes
oh yes
sign here
what was that again sir?
i was sold
not any sign
of service to see
i was however guided
quite kindly
to the extensive
t&cs

it's a promise
of the good stuff
it definitely is
we've taken the raw
mixed it
bashed it
added a bit more
we've even kept the rough
because that's
where the goodness
really is
the smooth is
almost always
a ruse
it's like
when they
sold you booze
it was never
going to end
not in good news
like your father smoked
and his
grandfather chewed
your friend
with the vape
they won't escape
what they sold you
starring at the screen
like heroin
but sort of clean
it's a promise
[of the good stuff]
that keeps us keen

tax return day
is a more coffee day
pick up the guitar
more often day
pop down for a snack
things like that
doing them a lot
anything but
you know what
day

happy new year
a time to cheer
a promise to exercise
and drink less beer
and then a promise
to keep it this time
unlike last year!

ok so
it's almost done
soon another
i will have begun
if i carry on this way
i'll put on some weight
and my new year
will have to start
with
a run

not any?
well not alive?
what if they
dare tread
where
his ghost
strides?
new songs
and old
for one day
it will be told
that a one
from today
will be too
as great
and ancient
sold

*in answer to a question, can there be any other
bards than Robert Burns on New year? written 31-
12-2023*

the day
it all became clear
the day
it was obvious really
that nothing is
not really
sure
other than
that is
that people
feel
and hurt
and wonder
have minds of their own
and may contradict
they are rarely alone
they
may not know
what you know
or as much
or understand
as such
or may have woken up
to a different dawn
as they mowed their lawn
and you watched
a robot
mow your own

i know
i have
this habit
of keeping
it brief
to many
many
few
i know
that's quite
a relief

if you
lie a lot
no one
will believe you
when
you're not

shallow
is mostly
how we present
there isn't
deep meaning
in every event
though
little things
here and there
build up
to mighty mounds
of why we are here

i
ai
the creator
of i?
or
am i?
i

no wifi
well almost
and to get
a phone signal
i have to climb a post
so quiet
i can hear the cows moo
you'd say bliss
and mostly
i'd say true
but home
is home
and the kids
want to use their phones
so considering that
to keep their
sanity intact
we should stay
longer than planned
for
at least a day
or two

i might not write today
the kids are over excited
and i don't think
i will have time to write it

merry christmas

it's the last build up
everyone is anxious
it's really really
nearly here
there will certainly be
the odd mix up
but it's so precious
when all the neighbours
come together
without discourse
but no one knows
not really
not for sure
which days
are bin days
because it's never clear
in the last week
of the year

the imposter
reads one book
and believes it
the authentic
reads many
and has doubts
so don't be too sure
if they are too sure
but if you are not
you are probably
not far out

as the year
almost
comes to a close
we could draw a line
under it
you'd think
yet
so much
keeps happening
to keep me
on my toes

you never know
the last time you do
the last time
you see them
the last visit there
it could be tomorrow
or it could be done
the last time
you had this much fun
with someone

people will disagree
about God
about sport
about the how
the who
and of course
about poetry
but mostly agree
about good
mostly perhaps
except
the
me
me
me
needy
and
the greedy

the wind
that passes through
sometimes leaves
you happy
as the leaves dance
to a melody
and when it leaves
it's like a friend
you will miss
till they come again
other times the wind
it annoys
often destroys
flowers and others
lose their heads
and you simply don't want to come out
of bed
so no matter
if today
you are the wind
please
be the former
not the latter

shopping
the crowds
it means
i have to pop out
what if
oh what if
i'm found out
and they stop to chat
what do i chat about?
i'll stumble on words
maybe talk too loud
and stand out
too much
in the crowd

my noel
list
to do
i asked my
daughter
for me
to do
as my head
every thought
that passes through
is a little fuzzy
and
is followed
by an
achoo

my legs are a wobble
i'm sure i feel
a sniffle
and my head is adrift
i know this
means trouble
it happens often
at the time of year
for gifts
the neighbours
are the same
and so are the kids
the pharmacies
have no issue
though
nor do those
who make tissues
this time of year
always
gives them a lift

as i write
i mostly
tell a story
it's rarely about me
and not often true
but as i write
i see it from
the narrator
or the character's point of view
so
for every poem
every song
it's not me for long
but me
as long

*written in response to a question, are you ever
inside the character, you are writing when you
write?*

there's a fly
in my coffee
if i hadn't looked
it'd probably
now be in me
so
obviously
this must have
happened before
so
if i make another coffee
will i be looking at it
anxiously
constantly?

i nearly sat down
and wrote a verse
i've written before
nearly
but i still sat down
tired
it's been a long day
you may
know the score

the heart
it pumps the blood
it rules the head
but don't
tell a physician
this
is what i said

rush
not in a rush
well i am a bit
i've got
something else to do
several somethings
some need
some want
i'll probably need wings
but
i'll never be ahead
nor do i want to
so a head rush
as my mind says
too much!
then
everything
all at once
comes to

alarm
i set an alarm
it's an arbitrary time
and i didn't
give it a name
i must have
set it in a rush
now
i can ignore and maybe
it'll all be fine
then after again maybe
someone will complain
then i will blush
a bit
but hopefully
no one will come to any
harm

disguised
a lot of you are
or should i say us
i'm sure you realise
in truth
it's everyone of us
who really knows
how anyone is
in their head
some
true
are more true
and they end up
being more talked about
by me and you
so we hide
and only drip drip
bits of what's inside

writer
poet
and the
mistermed
stoic
songwriter
lyricist
and
rhymer
be you a
pen smith
of kind
proser
or prosaic
carry on
please
till
your tomorrow
does not
come

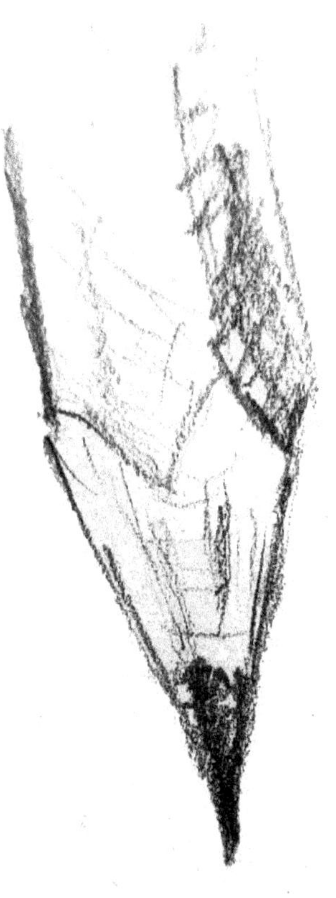

presence
more than
presents
if you
really mean it
and
feel it

prejudice
is a disease
born
out of ill belief
of thoughts
ill conceived
we all have them
probably
a little bit
for some though
it's quite a lot
souls lost
in the unhappiness
they bring
to both them
and their victims

some say
poems
are for writers
who don't like
to write a lot
i think
not

the problem with
the so called market square
when laid bare
is that the rough
and the loud
and normally the nasty
have the crowd
the quiet
and the humble
who are often the wisest
do not
those with money
trump those without
the fair
and the kind
rarely
get a shout

we are told these days
call out the bullsh*t
last time i tried it
i was gaslit
but i was dealing
with a narcissist
my empathy
verses something empty
how does anyone
deal with it?

i thought i had
an hour clear
sounds like
the whole world heard
so they decided
that's a good
time to call
so my coffee went cold
my kitkat half chewed
and in the end
i had no time at all

use any medium
i remember
that's what it said
the art exam question
after a one liner
most just put
pen to paper
though some used paint
others just paper
don't be scared
to be considered
medium or mediocre
if it means
music
words
moving pictures
or tapioca
anything
just
free your soul
never hand it over

the ordinary world
the one that's
not ordinary folk
the one that's
painted
rehearsed
with prewritten jokes
it pays
yes indeed it does
even though
it can let you thrive
and feel your buzz
this ordinary world
once they are done
will spit you out
like chewed gum
so remember if you can
do all you can
to have some fun
and while you are at it
don't hurt
anyone

it's a doom scroll
on social media
for many
on tiktok
facebook
and X
(formerly twitter)
it feeds the anxious
and the bitter
and one
leads to the other
but not here it seems
on threads
we juiced the algo
with rhyme
and rhythm
and we got fed
lots of poetry
instead

a break
this time
i chose coffee
later it might be
chocolate
or tea
the dr
says water
and nothing fizzy
i need a break
midmorning
like anybody
but if i put the brake
on my coffee
will it break me?

memories
sometimes
are unkind
some
sparkle
and cuddle
sometimes
our minds

a dark hot chocolate
a sausage roll
a packet of crisps
and magazine
time to forget
for a bit
untangling my hair
a mind stroll
bliss

the countdown begins
the excitement
i can't rein it in
the truck will be here
to empty the bins

last night
i watched a play
about the war
to end all wars
my daughter played a minor part
she was great
they all were
but that's not what this is about
my grandfather was born
2 years before that war was done
my mother
his daughter
was born 3 days before the next one
and her dad for a while was gone
he was lucky to survive
but not long enough
to see me much alive as
from what i understand
in 1945 he was very much undone
to end all wars
home by christmas
still too many
wont be home
by this one

i didn't write
a thing today
though my mind
was much at play
words came as i walked
and as i talked
with friends
at the café
as i worked too
but as soon as i
brought my mind to
nothing!
though i am sure
earlier
in the outside
and in the pause of thought
yes
i'm pretty sure
i had much
much to say

no matter
whatever i say
i'm screwed
if i agree
with them
or you
or neither
then too
if i say
i am red
or i'm blue
if i am white or black
or a little bit of this and that
so i plead not
yet i agree
words matter indeed
but only it seems
if i say the right ones
for you

it's in a safe place
but i've looked
in all my safe places
i can't find it
i knew the moment
i tidied up
my so called mess
in haste
i'd never find anything
ever again
yes we've all
heard this song
give me
a chest of drawers
and i'll fill it
with things
my children will find
when they clean up
when i'm gone
i'm in my safe place
i can see all my things
my prompts
my wings
am i wrong?

just write
let it all out
even
if in the end
it means
nowt

apparently
the brain enjoys
a deep long sleep
mine has had
a lot of fun
apparently
lately
it enjoys it
when i am chatting
thinking
or reading
apparently tho'
i can talk too much
sorry
i know
what was i thinking?
because of it
apparently
everybody knows
so
thank you
for reading

genius
doesn't shine
like a show
not always
anyhow
yet it's
all around tho'
maybe even
at least a little
in everyone
genius
it's not what you know
if you figure it out
inside
you'll glow

the glory mile
we rarely credit
the drivers
but those
who took
the ride

seize the day
they said
well
look how that
ended up
well
i'll get up
next time
watch
the birds eat the worms
and
spiders eat the flies
they can have
tomorrow

toast or cereal
sometimes
that's the hardest choice
coffee or tea
that one's easy
well you'd think it would be
sometimes
if i am lucky
that's the hardest choice

noise

can you imagine it?
if all we were thinking
was making it
computers read
each others' minds
what a bind we'd be in
if it were for all
human kind

obvious things really
when we are born
for a moment
we are the same
when we are dead
we are dead
just the same
on our journey
some of us
will have found fame
some will have done more
and better
but you wont
know their names
some will have died because another
decides
because of their anger
lust for wealth or power
but none
makes them happy
not really

run

run
run down
run down
sleeping
run
run
run down
the hill
where there's fighting
they will die there
for a cause
and they'll get
nothing
so
run
run
before they
run you down

when i press record
i freeze
before that
i play
with ease

faking it
it's something we do
almost every time
we say hello
and how do you do
yet when you wear
your heart on your sleeve
and we see you
it's way too much fuss
for us all
to go through
so to keep the calm
faking it
is what we do

if i try grab your
attention
and it's
something worthy
well at least
worthy to me
is it my self worth
i'm inflating
or am sharing selflessly?
it's hard to say
if it's at your expense
then i should recompense
sometimes
when i come knocking
say something clumsy
perhaps too naughty
i may
just want to play
not looking
for a scuffle
or debating

when the sun shines
the day
is mine
when it rains
i feel happy
for the trees
but they've been happy
a long time
today
the day
is mine

i've changed my mind
it happens a lot
new things fall
into my pot
it changes my stew
which changes my view
sometimes it's edible
though often
not

join us
joyous
in a happy word parade
only word i can think of
that rhymes
is lemonade
unless you count what eggs do
and folks
in an overly joyous mood

*a feel good thread, by threads, request written
in response*

sometimes
you forget
you are alive
and sometimes
so do i
we flog people
like some do horses
neither of which are right
just so we can get by
sometimes
we forget
we are all alive

some of us
are ghosts
i don't believe in ghosts
yet some of us
still are
i see you
i promise
even if
no one takes notice
i know who you are

we wonder a lot
what people think
but what's true
is they rarely do
well at least
not about you
they're
too tied up in the knot
of what others think of them
too

we say
never again
and yet
again
and
again

it's 10 past
i said
hurry
no it's 6 minutes past she said
mine says 8
said another
i think mine's fast
i said
she said
i'm sure mine's slow
i sync mine online
said another
oh wait
it's 10 past now
that's what i said
i said

i'll put on
some music today
put it up real loud
then every now and then
when i need a moment
and the right
song comes on
instead of a coffee
i'll stand up
and pretend
i'm playing
to a crowd

yes indeed
whatever it is
book or
ingredients' list
read a lot
write a bit

in reply to a writer telling people to read

ah cynicism
i thought you'd gone
but you were with us
all along
hiding in the shadows
of the kindness
the friendly exchanges
of book talk and poetry
humour and humanity
i'd self flagellated
for so long
i'd forgotten even
how to be
so wrong
cynicism
you have saved me
[Not!]

in response to a cynical view of writers
connecting on threads, by a writer!

so it's wet
so what?
the trees
need this
a lot
2023
record breaking hot
so it's wet today
what would happen
if it was always not?

500g

this plumber thing
it got me thinking
when they seek solace
after a hard day's work
it's often
an artist
a writer
a filmmaker
or poet
maybe
songwriter
singer
a creator of sorts
definitely
in a film
a book
a painting
a song
even all together
in a reel
15 seconds
long
so
just as important to them
as what they did
for someone
earlier on

*written in response after someone wrote that an
artist is a profession like being a plumber,
just not as important!*

as a
designer
creator
painter
a
poet
composer
writer
in
science
art
literature
or whatever
if you see
i've shown you just
one thing today
100 others
i've thrown away

stay in your lane
they said
but i have a brain
i said
i have a good degree
and an MSc
from a top university
not that that should matter
we can study
we can practice
if we try
we can be better
do more
keeping the grey matter
active
i can be an artist
engineer
scientist
and singer
a poet
a cook
a left or
right winger
i can read
i can think
i feel
and i love
but even love can
sometimes
have rage
but i will never try make you feel
small
even as i fall
i will get up
and read it all
every page

today
i see the sun
as i
saw you
it was like
you could fly
now i feel
so can i

you should see me
not hide
behind our thumbs
typing
see my eyes
my hands
scratching my brow
our bodies talking
as we laugh
or row
in silence
a smile
a breath
a stare
you should see me
else one day
it might be rare

when i woke up
this morning
i had some words
in my head
i should have
rushed out of bed
and written them down
but the kids woke up
and life was stretching
it's arms out
and yawning
this was far from
a lazy sunday morning
we had coffee
the kids had
not sure i noticed
one was
playing guitar already
and the other at her mother moaning
so nothing rhymes
and the words aren't really floating
whatever they were
this morning
words gone like time
yes
i should have
rushed out of bed

we don't ask
enough questions
i think
we are also
too quick to answer
i think
we shouldn't
answer them all
or any
if we don't think
i think
we all need
to look more
listen more
pause more
i think
if only we had the time
to think!

i have written
this before
every day it means
even more
vengeance
will chew you whole
and spit you out empty
your heart will be cold
and you will
have become
your enemy
better to show love
when faced with
adversity
more chance
of getting some back
than any

it takes a moment
to believe
yet a lifetime
to understand
only to learn
that what we believed
was wrong
the problem is
we told everyone
and it's hard
to make it undone

do you know
who i am?
i am no better
no more than you
we are the same
i may have a nice scarf
and you shiny shoes
we are the same

we enjoy the calm
as it's so rare
so much going on
normally
there's little
time to spare
[to be] serene
it's more of *a* wish
or a memory
so enjoy the calm
when it's there

almost half a ton
yeah man
if that's bad verse
i've heard
so much worse

written on reaching 498 followers on threads

morning
be good
when i asked yesterday
not sure
you understood
ok
try again tomorrow
i need sleep
but not to keep
anyone got some
i can borrow?

31.10.2023
we were trick'd
the outcome's fixed
they said
well you
would go to vegas
as a treat
so don't bleat

when you're
playing badminton
the opposition is playing tennis
this is just how life is
marmite comes in a jar
that's simple
but both beer and mars
are bought in bars
if you're not too confused
some small people
wear very large shoes
some feel
to others that makes no sense
yet logic
is always defied
it too
has more than one side
this is just how life is

feel everything
till
everything
numbs

infinity
was never on the cards
nor was i
that's twice they lied
so i won't take them
seriously

when i start
a bit of verse on here
i have no idea
what i will write next
nor the context
nor when
i end

a normal day?
no such thing
i wake up and
things
things
things

i cannot conjure
if i'm held under

war
why?
people just
die
others make money
not funny

we're all dancing
we copy the first
unless of course
they're the worst
mind you
if they're smiling the most
then...

today i hear every noise
soaked in adrenalin
i can't find poise
i still
hear every noise

the kids are home
and it's quiet
they used to run riot
playing with
plastic toys
i loved the noise
i hope it's homework
or they're reading books or something
if i turn the wifi off will they run
to me moaning?

is i
ai?
am i?
so i could be an ai
but i am not sure
my spelling suggests
i am not
my indifference suggests
i might be
my incoherence
definitely implies
otherwise

the forever
changing wind
blows harder
from the east
then the west
over
and under
i am the leaf
caught
taken wherever

love

=

proximity
could be creepy ofc.
distance
is worse
unless you're
a bit of a psycho
then
that could be
also

sometimes
it's time
to write
but mostly
it's time
to read
listen
and after that
it's time
to think
sometimes
after that
it's time
to write
mostly
it's not

read a little
affirm your beliefs
read a lot
destroy them
actually
i probably mean prejudices
don't i?
this time
i'll let it
fly

we wait
standing at
the school gate
when they're
running late
for food
for love
for the next
episode to land
if only all of it
was on demand
but then
would life be too fast?
would the good stuff last less long?
again
for love
better to wait a little
than have it always
to hand

fog of hate
at an exponential rate
anger mounts
and we shout
and we shout
we hear nothing
but
we shout

the day
starts
staring at the garden with a cup of
coffee watching the squirrels and the
robot mower affectionately called
mowanna
by the girls
play
as so many
school mottos
say in latin
seize the day
looks like
it's taken though! coffee's getting
cold

if
we didn't watch
the news
read other
people's views
not have to have an opinion on
everything
listen to music loud
and think of nothing
but what's happening
down the road
at the village school
what would we lose?

it's all new
yes but we all get bored of **the Parody**
eventually
it never breaks us free
if this was once the town square it is
now a circus
and everyone's
the freakshow
no one really says hello
intellectual discourse
is naught
and every battle
is drone on drone
the truth is
you're alone

this was written on twitter before closing my account